The European Union

Political, Social, and Economic Cooperation

THE
EUROPEAN UNION

POLITICAL, SOCIAL, AND ECONOMIC COOPERATION

The European Union

Political, Social, and Economic Cooperation

MALTA

by
James Stafford

Mason Crest Publishers
Philadelphia

Mason Crest Publishers Inc.
370 Reed Road, Broomall, Pennsylvania 19008
(866) MCP-BOOK (toll free)
www.masoncrest.com

First printing
1 2 3 4 5 6 7 8 9 10

        Library of Congress Cataloging-in-Publication Data

Stafford, James, 1963-
  Malta / by James Stafford.
      p. cm.—(The European Union: political, social, and economic cooperation)
  Includes index.
    ISBN 1-4222-0056-6
    ISBN 1-4222-0038-8 (series)
  1. Malta—Juvenile literature. 2. European Union—Malta—Juvenile literature. I. Title. II. European Union (Series) (Philadelphia, Pa.)
  DG989.S82 2006
  945.8'5—dc22
                                2005020325

Produced by Harding House Publishing Service, Inc.
www.hardinghousepages.com
Interior design by Benjamin Stewart.
Cover design by MK Bassett-Harvey.
Printed in the Hashemite Kingdom of Jordan.

CONTENTS

MALTA

European Union Member since 2004

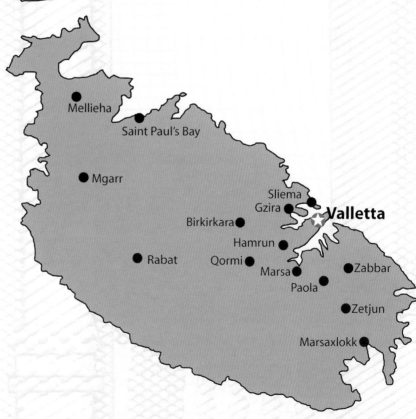

Gharb

Victoria

Nadur

Mgarr

Comino

Mellieha

Saint Paul's Bay

Mgarr

Sliema

Gzira

Valletta

Birkirkara

Hamrun

Qormi

Rabat

Marsa

Zabbar

Paola

Zetjun

Marsaxlokk

INTRODUCTION

Sixty years ago, Europe lay scarred from the battles of the Second World War. During the next several years, a plan began to take shape that would unite the countries of the European continent so that future wars would be inconceivable. On May 9, 1950, French Foreign Minister Robert Schuman issued a declaration calling on France, Germany, and other European countries to pool together their coal and steel production as "the first concrete foundation of a European federation." "Europe Day" is celebrated each year on May 9 to commemorate the beginning of the European Union (EU).

The EU consists of twenty-five countries, spanning the continent from Ireland in the west to the border of Russia in the east. Eight of the ten most recently admitted EU member states are former communist regimes that were behind the Iron Curtain for most of the latter half of the twentieth century.

Any European country with a democratic government, a functioning market economy, respect for fundamental rights, and a government capable of implementing EU laws and policies may apply for membership. Bulgaria and Romania are set to join the EU in 2007. Croatia and Turkey have also embarked on the road to EU membership.

While the EU began as an idea to ensure peace in Europe through interconnected economies, it has evolved into so much more today:

- Citizens can travel freely throughout most of the EU without carrying a passport and without stopping for border checks.

- EU citizens can live, work, study, and retire in another EU country if they wish.

- The euro, the single currency accepted throughout twelve of the EU countries (with more to come), is one of the EU's most tangible achievements, facilitating commerce and making possible a single financial market that benefits both individuals and businesses.

- The EU ensures cooperation in the fight against cross-border crime and terrorism.

- The EU is spearheading world efforts to preserve the environment.

- As the world's largest trading bloc, the EU uses its influence to promote fair rules for world trade, ensuring that globalization also benefits the poorest countries.

- The EU is already the world's largest donor of humanitarian aid and development assistance, providing 55 percent of global official development assistance to developing countries in 2004.

The EU is neither a nation intended to replace existing nations, nor an international organization. The EU is unique—its member countries have established common institutions to which they delegate some of their sovereignty so that decisions on matters of joint interest can be made democratically at the European level.

Europe is a continent with many different traditions and languages, but with shared values such as democracy, freedom, and social justice, cherished values well known to North Americans. Indeed, the EU motto is "United in Diversity."

Enjoy your reading. Take advantage of this chance to learn more about Europe and the EU!

Ambassador John Bruton,
Head of Delegation of the European Commission, Washington, D.C.

Malta's Azur Window

CHAPTER 1 THE LANDSCAPE

Malta is an **archipelago** made of **coralline** limestone in the central Mediterranean Sea. Its central location amid other Mediterranean countries, as well as its numerous natural harbors, have given it a location of strategic importance for thousands of years. It is 58 miles (93 kilometers) south of Sicily and 186 miles (300 kilometers) north of Africa, and its size is 122 square miles (316 square kilometers)—a little less than twice the size of

Washington, D.C. Malta's largest islands, which are also the only inhabited ones, are Malta, Gozo, and Comino. Malta is the largest of these islands, measuring seventeen miles (27 kilometers) at its longest point from northwest to south-

QUICK FACTS: THE GEOGRAPHY OF MALTA

Location: southern Europe, islands in the Mediterranean Sea, south of Sicily
Area: slightly less than twice the size of Washington, D.C.
  total: 122 square miles (316 sq. km.)
  land: 122 square miles (316 sq. km.)
  water: NA
Borders: NA
Climate: Mediterranean with mild, rainy winters and hot, dry summers
Terrain: mostly low, rocky, flat to dissected plains; many coastal cliffs
Elevation extremes:
  lowest point: Mediterranean Sea—0 feet (0 meters)
  highest point: Ta'Dmejrek—830 feet (253 meters)
Natural hazards: NA

Source: www.cia.org, 2005

sea, the yellow of the limestone, the red of the soil, and the green of the olive and **carob trees**. The terrain is low and rocky, with plains in the central areas of the islands and large cliffs on the coasts. The rocky terrain has been said to look like some of the drier parts of Greece, with thin soil over limestone, dwarf vegetation, and many drought-resistant plants. However, the island of Gozo is a bit greener than the island of Malta because of its blue clay subsoil. The coastlines of all the islands are indented and very sheltered, with spectacular cliffs, home to hundreds of species of wildlife and birds. Many of these cliffs drop 820 feet (250 meters) straight down to the sea.

Because, there are no rivers or lakes on any of the islands, and also because the rainfall averages only twenty-three inches (578 mm) per year, water has always been scarce in the coun-

east, and nine miles (14.5 kilometers) at its widest point from west to east. Gozo is one-third the size of Malta, but is more lush, with deep green valleys and more farming and fishing than the larger island. Comino, smaller still, is mostly used for swimming, snorkeling, and windsurfing. It is known for its clear waters and blue lagoons.

The landscape of Malta is very colorful, especially from the air. Colors include the blue of the try, and farming has been presented with many challenges. Ancient stone walls that cross the fields were built to retain topsoil. The hillsides are terraced to increase farming areas, and the prickly pear cactus—that has now spread everywhere over the island—still marks boundaries between fields as it has for centuries. Although the brief winter storms fill reservoirs and **cisterns** on the island, providing some irrigation for the fields, the modern

The Salt Marsh at Qbajjar

View of Malta's landscape

islands now depend on five modern **desalination plants** that convert salt water into freshwater.

Malta has a typical Mediterranean climate with two main seasons: mild, rainy winters and hot, dry summers. Plant life, therefore, has had to adapt itself to these two drastic extremes. From mid-November until mid-May, the islands are green and lush, with fields of vegetables on the south of the island of Malta, and colorful spots covered with fennel, clover, wild iris, myrtle, and over 1,000 other wild species of plants.

Farmers on the northern and southern parts of the large island and also on Gozo still use traditional farming methods, with their village life revolving around the seasons of fishing and farming. The center of the large island contains resorts and cities, while its northern area is a more barren variety of farmland, with goats and sheep often seen along roadways.

The only forested area on any of the islands is Buskett Gardens, planted in the seventeenth century by the Knights of St. John as a hunting ground. Native plants of the islands include olive trees, carob trees, fig trees, the evergreen oak, and the wild almond. Hundreds of years ago, eucalyptus and evergreen trees were planted to provide shade and protection for fields and houses. Within the last fifty years, decorative flowering trees have been introduced, such as hibiscus, oleander, tamarisk, jacaranda, the flame-pink Judas tree, and the yellow mimosa.

The ocean plays a vital role in Malta's natural environment.

The islands are also home to many small wild animals, like hedgehogs, lizards, snakes, weasels, and bats. Many water birds live near the floodplain of muddy water near the northern coast. These include grebes, moorhen, kingfishers, and herons. Malta's national bird is the rare blue rock thrush, which nests in its southern cliffs. Also, over 350 species of birds that migrate from Northern Europe to Africa have been spotted as they have stopped over at the islands.

Reminders of Malta's past are seen around the Grand Harbour in Vittoriosa.

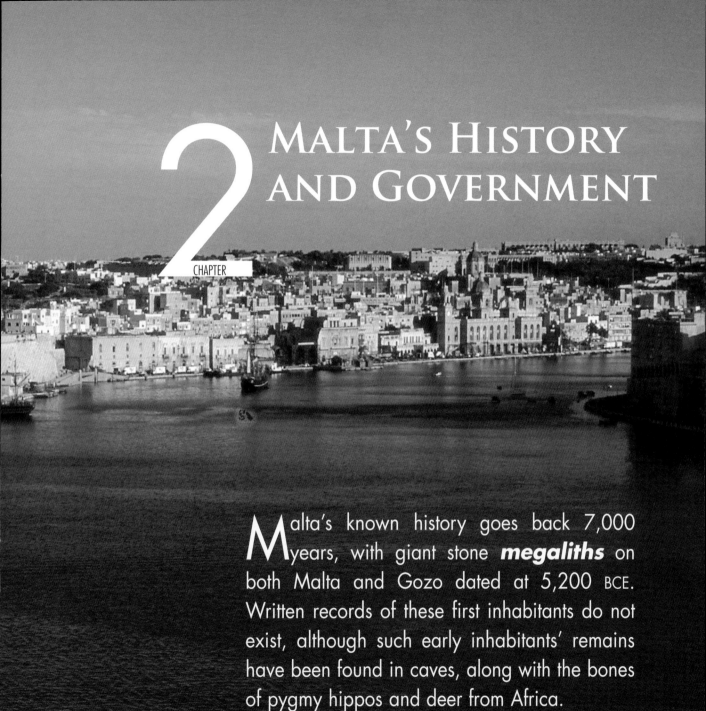

2 MALTA'S HISTORY AND GOVERNMENT

CHAPTER

Malta's known history goes back 7,000 years, with giant stone **megaliths** on both Malta and Gozo dated at 5,200 BCE. Written records of these first inhabitants do not exist, although such early inhabitants' remains have been found in caves, along with the bones of pygmy hippos and deer from Africa.

DATING SYSTEMS AND THEIR MEANING

You might be accustomed to seeing dates expressed with the abbreviations BC or AD, as in the year 1000 BC or the year AD 1900. For centuries, this dating system has been the most common in the Western world. However, since BC and AD are based on Christianity (BC stands for Before Christ and AD stands for *anno Domini*, Latin for "in the year of our Lord"), many people now prefer to use abbreviations that people from all religions can be comfortable using. The abbreviations BCE (meaning Before Common Era) and CE (meaning Common Era) mark time in the same way (for example, 1000 BC is the same year as 1000 BCE, and AD 1900 is the same year as 1900 CE), but BCE and CE do not have the same religious overtones as BC and AD.

Settlers from Sicily, an Italian island off the coast of southern Europe, arrived around 5000 BCE, and raised pigs, cattle, sheep, and goats, as well as barley and wheat. Over the following cen-

WHO WAS SAINT PAUL?

Paul was a first-century Christian who was responsible for writing much of the New Testament, as well as spreading Christianity throughout the Mediterranean world.

turies, several other Mediterranean groups arrived, including the Phoenicians (ancient dwellers of Lebanon and Syria) in 800 BCE. The Phoenicians were traders who used the island as a stopping place in their voyages. The Carthaginians (from Northern Africa) then colonized the islands during the eighth century BCE.

The various peoples of Malta enjoyed peace until the Punic Wars between Rome and Carthage erupted. During the first war, from 262 to 242 BCE, Malta served as a naval base for Carthage. Then finally, captured by Rome, Malta became a Roman colony from 218 BCE until the fifth century CE. It is said that Saint Paul himself was shipwrecked on the island around 60 CE.

During the period of Rome's rule, the Maltese achieved Roman citizenship, became known for their quality textiles, and continued to speak the Phoenician language until the Arab conquest of 870. The Romans also built many limestone forts on the islands, especially around the cities of Mdina and Rabat.

Malta then became part of the Germanic kingdoms and, along with the Italian island of Sicily, was ruled by the Vandals and Visigoths in the fifth century. The Muslims who invaded and overtook the islands in 870 introduced citrus fruits, cotton, and irrigation. French-speaking Normans successfully invaded in 1090 and built some churches, although most residents still practiced Islam in the eleventh and twelfth centuries.

Malta's St. Paul's Bay

The Hagar Qim Temples are more than 5,000 years old.

In 1282, Peter of Aragon, a Spanish king, controlled both Malta and Sicily. He soon awarded the islands to his noble followers, mostly Sicilian nobles. However, by the 1420s, it became expensive for Spain to defend the islands against the **plague**, the raids of Muslim pirates, and invaders from northern Africa who arrived to steal property and to enslave the inhabitants.

In 1530, the king of Spain gave Malta to the Knights of the Order of St. John of Jerusalem for the yearly rent of one Maltese falcon. The knights built the large, fortified city of Valletta to protect against Muslim raids. The knights governed the island until 1798, when Napoleon Bonaparte of France took the island.

The British then blockaded the island against the arrival of French ships, and claimed it as their own naval base from 1814 until 1964. As a British naval base, the island was a target for both German and Italian bombing attacks during World War II. At this point, English became the dominant language of the island, although the structure of the government in relation to Britain changed several times during the years of British rule.

In 1921, Malta became self-governing, with power shared between British and Maltese ministers. In 1936, Malta became a colony of Britain, and in 1964, Malta became independent within the larger British Commonwealth. It became a **republic** in 1974, and was finally completely free of Britain in 1979 when it claimed its neutrality.

WHO WERE THE VANDALS AND THE VISIGOTHS?

The Vandals were a Germanic people that overran Gaul, Spain, and northern Africa in the fourth and fifth centuries CE; they sacked Rome in 455 CE. The Visigoths were members of the western Goths who invaded the Roman Empire in the fourth century CE and settled in France and Spain, ruling until the early eighth century.

WHO WAS NAPOLEON BONAPARTE?

Napoleon Bonaparte was the emperor of France from 1804 to 1814 who conquered much of Europe but was then forced from the throne.

The medieval gate to the town of Vittoriosa

Today, Malta is a **parliamentary democracy**. A president is appointed by parliament. The president in turn appoints a prime minister, usually the person who is the leader of the political party with the majority of seats in the House of Representatives. The president also appoints individual ministers to each of the governmental departments. The president's cabinet is selected from among members of the House of Representatives, a body that has between sixty-five and sixty-nine members and is based on proportional representation. Elections are held every five years.

Malta's **judiciary** system is independent of the **executive** and **legislative** branches of government. The Chief Justice and sixteen judges are appointed by the president, with a retirement age of sixty-five for all justices. Malta's courts include a civil court, a commercial court, a family court, and a criminal court.

Within each criminal court is a judge and a jury of nine. The highest court, the Constitutional Court, has heard appeals on human rights' cases, interpretation of the **constitution**, and disputed parliamentary elections and corrupt **electoral** practices.

Even though the country has achieved democracy, tensions between political parties still divide the inhabitants. Within Malta's thirteen electoral districts, the main political parties are the Nationalist Party, the Malta Labor Party, and the Green Party. However, the Nationalist and Labor parties dominate, with the Green Party holding no

The Vigilance Symbol, a reminder of Malta's past

parliamentary seats since its creation in 1989. Of Malta's five representatives sent to the European Union Parliament, two are from the Nationalist Party, and three are from the Labor Party.

The busy town of Marsaxlokk

CHAPTER 3
THE ECONOMY

For 440 years, Malta was merely an economic property connected to Sicily, which was sold and resold to **feudal** lords and barons, rulers of Swabia, Aquitaine, Aragon, Castille, and Spain. However, since its declared independence in 1964, the country has made great economic strides, at first following a policy of close cooperation with the United Kingdom and other NATO countries, then actively participating in the United Nations, the Commonwealth, the Council of Europe, the Organization for Security and Co-operation in Europe (OSCE), and the Non-Aligned Movement. In 2004, Malta joined the European Union (EU), after a **referendum** the year before that found 53.6 percent of the voters in favor of the move; 46.4 percent were in favor of maintaining a completely independent Malta. Malta could now boast an even more favored status as a European trade partner.

Malta's main economic resources include its limestone (which is used as building material on the island), its central location in the Mediterranean, and its productive labor force. Its **literacy rate** has now reached 90 percent, compared to 63 percent in 1946. Also, one of its two major languages is English, the other being Maltese, which is a **Semitic** language. The country must use these advantages to offset its lack of any freshwater, the fact that it produces no energy, and that it grows only 20 percent of its food.

Since the mid-1980s, Malta has learned to depend on tourism. Its exports, especially **semiconductors** and textiles, are those that have benefited from its productive labor force. Other Maltese industries include shipbuilding and repair, food and beverage packaging, footwear, clothing, and tobacco.

As of 1999, the composition of Malta's workforce was 5 percent agriculture, 26 percent industry, and 71 percent service industries, with an unemployment

Quick Facts: The Economy of Malta

Gross Domestic Product (GDP): US$7.223 billion

GDP per capita: US$18,200

Industries: tourism, electronics, ship building and repair, construction; food and beverages, textiles, footwear, clothing, tobacco

Agriculture: potatoes, cauliflower, grapes, wheat, barley, tomatoes, citrus, cut flowers, green peppers; pork, milk, poultry, eggs

Export commodities: machinery and transport equipment, manufactures

Export partners: Singapore 15.5%, US 12%, France 10.5%, UK 10.1%, Germany 9%, China 5.8%

Import commodities: machinery and transport equipment, manufactured and semimanufactured goods; food, drink, and tobacco

Import partners: Italy 18.2%, France 17.9%, UK 9.7%, Germany 9.2%, Singapore 6.9%, China 5.7%

Currency: Maltese lira (MTL)

Currency exchange rate: US$1 = 0.35 MTL (July 13, 2005)

Note: All figures are from 2004 unless otherwise noted.
Source: www.cia.org, 2005.

Maltese fisherman

A lacemaker in Gozo

rate of only 5.5 percent. Since 1987, the government itself has invested in an extensive tourism program, and in 1999 alone, over 1 million tourists visited the island. Inflation has remained low during all these endeavors.

Even though the Nationalist and Labor parties are divided on most issues, the country's deficit is a continuing concern for everyone. As a result, the parliament as a whole has begun work to lessen the government's size, and therefore spending. Even so, the country's economy is still heavily government regulated. Although Malta has no local government bodies and few regional branches of its central government, government programs are still strictly administered directly from the capital city of Valletta.

The government's present attempt to reduce its regulation of industry is known as economic liberalization. This policy's goal is to let industry itself react to the circumstances of trade, and grow or shift in reaction to those circumstances. Similarly, the government has announced plans to reform the pension and welfare systems, reducing government involvement in those areas.

Although tourism has steadily increased since the 1970s, it fell 7 percent during 2001 and 2002 in reaction to the attack on the World Trade Center in the United States. Also, the worldwide falling off of high-tech markets has affected Malta's industry in recent years.

A city bus in Marsaxlokk

Malta's economy is also challenged by the islands' population density. It is one of the most densely populated countries in the world, with 3,000 people per square mile, as compared to 55 people per square mile in the United States. It is also one of the poorer EU countries, with an average income of $17,700 per person.

Malta's currency is the lira (LM), which is decimal based, divided into 100 cents. It hopes to adopt the euro, the currency of the EU, within the next few years.

Although the United States and Malta established full diplomatic relations of Malta's independence in 1964, Malta's government desires improved relations with the United States and Europe, for both more trade and private investment.

A small boat floats in the water beside the St. Lawrence Maritime Museum in Vittoriosa.

4 MALTA'S PEOPLE AND CULTURE

CHAPTER

Because of Malta's tumultuous past, both its culture and its people share a unique mix of ethnic influences. Although the appearance of the Maltese people themselves is distinctive, an observer can see aspects of Arab, Roman, Phoenician, Spanish, and Sicilian cultures.

Likewise, one can see a similar ethnic mixture within the honey-colored limestone architecture of the islands. The **Neolithic** people who lived on

From 870 to 1200, Arabs created a huge system of forts around the city of Mdina. The Aragonese, or Spanish, left 500-year-old enclosed wooden balconies on the buildings of their town centers. The Knights of St. John, who ruled for 268 years starting in the year 1530, built many beautiful cathedrals.

Much of the country's culture and social life still centers around the religion and churches established by the knights. Today, 87 percent of the residents of Malta are regular church-goers, the largest percentage of any European population, and 97 percent of the residents profess to be Roman Catholic. The Church, therefore, is pervasive within the daily lives of the citizens and provides a series of feasts and pageants for the residents of the islands throughout the year. Each village celebrates its own patron saint. These events usually feature colorful processions, *Ghana* (folksinging), the preparation of special foods (such as fried rabbit picnics), dancing, and fireworks. Football (soccer) is the nation's most popular sport and is often played at these celebrations by the younger crowd.

Some of the largest celebrations on Malta include Imnarja, the feast of St. Peter and St. Paul, Good Friday (a more solemn festival), and the Annual Carnival at the city of Valletta, which includes the dancing of the Parata, a sword dance commemorating the Maltese victory over the Turkish army in

Quick Facts: The People of Malta

Population: 398,534
Ethnic groups: Maltese
Age structure:
   0–14 years: 17.6%
   15–64 years: 68.8%
   65 years and over: 13.6%
Population growth rate: 0.42%
Birth rate: 10.17 births/1,000 pop.
Death rate: 8 deaths/1,000 pop.
Migration rate: 2.06 migrant(s)/1,000 pop.
Infant mortality rate: 3.89 deaths/1,000 live births
Life expectancy at birth:
   Total population: 78.86 years
   Male: 76.7 years
   Female: 81.15 years
Total fertility rate: 1.5 children born/woman
Religions: Roman Catholic 98%
Languages: Maltese (official), English (official)
Literacy rate: 93.6% (2003)

Note: All figures are from 2005 unless otherwise noted.
Source: www.cia.org, 2005.

the islands 5,000 years ago built huge temples to the gods, and the ruins are still visible today.

Women making lace in Gozo

1565. Carnival time, which occurs for three days in mid-February, precedes the beginning of Lent. This celebration extends from Valletta into every small town, where partiers wear clever masks to conceal their identities.

A celebrant at one of these events might follow a procession down the street of his parish, following a representation of the town's saint, which is usually carried shoulder high. Flags and banners adorn the streets, with children often throwing confetti from the balconies. Bands play. Bells ring. Houses are brightly lit, decorated inside and out, with their doors flung open, so that friends and relatives can enter to share food and to see the decorations. The village church is draped with red ***damask*** and decorated with flowers.

Street-corner shrines are everywhere, some of them finely carved, and some of them crude and brightly colored. The churches passed by the parade-goers have impressive domes and ***baroque*** architecture, the most famous of these being the sixteenth-century St. John's Cathedral in Valletta. Those who enter the churches find grand interiors, paintings, and ***frescoes***.

The food at Maltese celebrations varies with seasonal produce and the catches of fishermen, but there are also some favorite dishes. A thin pastry is often used to encase vegetables, cheese, fish, meat, rice, or pasta. Pastizzi, which is Turkish in origin, is small and boat-shaped, with ricotta cheese and egg wrapped within a thin pastry. Kannoli, from Sicily, is a tube-shaped dessert containing fruit or sweets.

Cathedral St. Jean, one of Malta's many churches

Maltese fishing boats often have eyes.

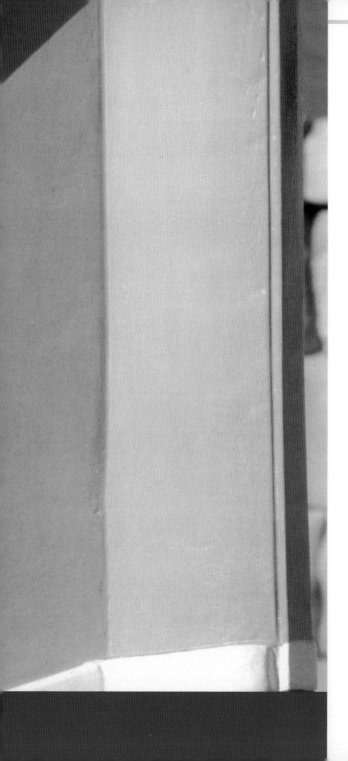

Despite the historical influences on the islands, the modern world also enters the daily lives of the Maltese people, whose population, in 2001, reached 394,583. There are two daily newspapers, one in Maltese and one in English. Privately run radio and television stations have existed since the 1990s. Maltese (a language similar to Arabic) and English are both official languages of the country, although Italian is widely spoken as well. The daily language of the people, which is Semitic in origin but written in Latin script with an alphabet of thirty letters, is said to date back to the early Phoenicians, making it one of the oldest languages in daily use. Education is now free within the country, and it is compulsory until age sixteen.

Within the modern world, there is often no clear distinction between the past and present cultures of Malta. Valletta, Malta's capital and largest cultural center, houses the National Museum of Archaeology, the Museum of Fine Arts, the War Museum, and the Manoel Theatre (which is the second oldest theatre in Europe).

The National Library of Malta contains a large eighteenth-century collection, as well as archives of the Knights of St. John. The University of Malta, with an enrollment of 5,000 students in 1994, originally opened its doors in 1592.

Even street vendors advertise their wares by singing traditional (Ghana) folksongs. Within the Ghana, background folk-guitar music plays while two or three people take turns arguing a point in a melodic voice.

Xewkija Church in Gozo

5

THE CITIES

Each of Malta's three major cities is located on the main island of Malta, and each showcases a specific set of events from the country's history. Valletta, Malta's capital city, lies on the northeast corner of the island, on the steep Scriberras Peninsula that juts out between two natural harbors. Constructed in 1565, the city was first inhabited by the Knights of St. John.

St. Elme Fortress in Valletta

Mdina, centrally located on the island of Malta, is a walled fortress first inhabited by the Phoenicians 3,000 years ago. And Rabat, the commercial center of Malta, is famous for both ruins and artifacts saved from the Roman occupation of the islands.

VALLETTA

Walls and huge **bastions** surround Valletta, and its streets are arranged in orderly grids. In 1565, the pope sent his own architect, Francesi Laparelli (who was also Michelangelo's assistant), to design the city. The purpose of the city was to protect the knights against Turkish invaders. The city was so well designed that it was never invaded, and its walls were never tested by attack.

The city was also a marvel of Renaissance planning principles, with streets laid out to channel cool breezes from the harbor. The street grids open up into squares full of impressive buildings at the center of the city.

Although Valletta was named after the founder of the Knights of St. John, Grandmaster Jean de Vallette, it has many nicknames. It has been called both "the Fortress," and "a city built by gentlemen for gentlemen." However, the Maltese themselves call it "*Il Belt*," which means "the City."

Valletta is both Malta's capital, a living, working city, and a city with a well-preserved history. For example, the narrow grids of tiny streets are filled with shops full of both historical and modern goods. At night, the fortress bastions and the city's baroque architecture are lit up by a multitude of modern floodlights.

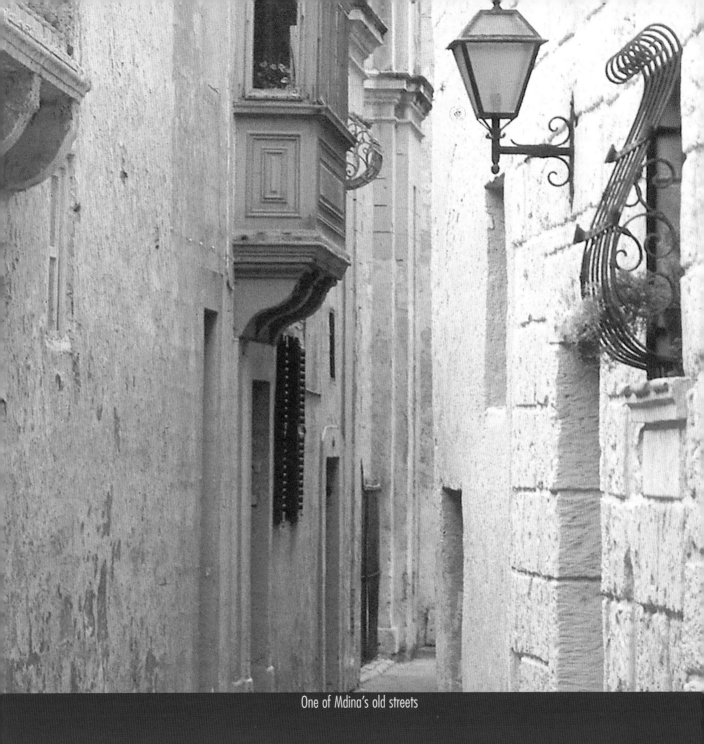

One of Mdina's old streets

The main sights of Valletta include the city's walls; the 500-year-old Grand Master's Palace, which takes up an entire city block and now houses Malta's parliament; and St. John's Cathedral, built in 1566 as the Knight's Church, with marble mosaic floors, a **lapis lazuli** altar, and tombstones built into the floor, commemorating knights of old.

People began to move away from Valletta and into the suburbs during World War II, when some damage was done to the city. The city lost its nineteenth-century opera house during bombing raids. Even so, the city hosts tourists from all over the globe, houses the government of Malta, and initiates many festivals of the island, including the Feasts of St. Paul, which are celebrated each year on February 10.

MDINA AND RABAT

Mdina and Rabat are two smaller, less populated, but nevertheless historically important cities. Because both these cities are much older than Valletta, they have Arabic rather than European names. *Mdina* means "city" or "town," and *Rabat* means "the suburb." Mdina and Rabat were once a single ancient city until the Saracens separated them by a wall in 870.

Both Mdina and Rabat are in the center of Malta, in an area of hills, farms, and smaller towns. Because the island of Malta is so small, both cities are merely nine miles (14 kilometers) west of the city of Valletta.

The main gate of Mdina

Mdina is located on a high plateau, overlooking the entire island, and it is older than Valletta; people have lived there for 4,000 years. The Phoenicians were among the first people to settle there. Because of Mdina's long history, its name has also changed many times, depending on each current ruler. The Romans took control of the city and based their own government of Malta there for several hundred years. Later, in the eleventh century, a beautiful Roman Catholic church was built in the city's main plaza. Mdina today is a quiet city that rests on many layers of history. Tourists still enter the city by drawbridge to find their way through the ancient cobblestone streets of the city.

Rabat, which is today the commercial center of central Malta, was once part of the Roman city of Melita, the city that was split into Rabat and Mdina when the Saracens built a thick wall around Mdina in 870. Today, Rabat is much livelier than Mdina; it is known for its Roman ruins, and also for the Christian catacombs, burial chambers that stretch for miles beneath the city. The Cathedral of St. Paul is reportedly built over the stone **grotto** where St. Paul stayed in the year 60, when he was shipwrecked on Malta.

The EU flag

6 THE FORMATION OF THE EUROPEAN UNION

The EU is an economic and political confederation of twenty-five European nations. Member countries abide by common foreign and security policies and cooperate on judicial and domestic affairs. The confederation, however, does not replace existing states or governments. Each of the twenty-five member states is **autonomous**, but they have all agreed to establish some common institutions and to hand over some of their own decision-making powers to these international bodies. As a result, decisions on matters that interest all member states can be made democratically, accommodating everyone's concerns and interests.

Today, the EU is the most powerful regional organization in the world. It has evolved from a primarily economic organization to an increasingly political one. Besides promoting economic cooperation, the EU requires that its members uphold fundamental values of peace and **solidarity**, human dignity, freedom, and equality. Based on the principles of democracy and the rule of law, the EU respects the culture and organizations of member states.

HISTORY

The seeds of the EU were planted more than fifty years ago in a Europe reduced to smoking piles of rubble by two world wars. European nations suffered great financial difficulties in the postwar period. They were struggling to get back on their feet and realized that another war would cause further hardship. Knowing that internal conflict was hurting all of Europe, a drive began toward European cooperation.

France took the first historic step. On May 9, 1950 (now celebrated as Europe Day), Robert Schuman, the French foreign minister, proposed the coal and steel industries of France and West Germany be coordinated under a single supranational authority. The proposal, known as the Treaty

of Paris, attracted four other countries—Belgium, Luxembourg, the Netherlands, and Italy—and resulted in the 1951 formation of the European Coal and Steel Community (ECSC). These six countries became the founding members of the EU.

In 1957, European cooperation took its next big leap. Under the Treaty of Rome, the European Economic Community (EEC) and the European Atomic Energy Community (EURATOM) were formed. Informally known as the Common Market, the EEC promoted joining the national economies into a single European economy. The 1965 Treaty of Brussels (more commonly referred to as the Merger Treaty) united these various treaty organizations under a single umbrella, the European Community (EC).

In 1992, the Maastricht Treaty (also known as the Treaty of the European Union) was signed in Maastricht, the Netherlands, signaling the birth of the EU as it stands today. **Ratified** the following year, the Maastricht Treaty provided for a central banking system, a common currency (the euro) to replace the national currencies, a legal definition of the EU, and a framework for expanding the

The EU's united economy has allowed it to become a worldwide financial power.

EU's political role, particularly in the area of foreign and security policy.

By 1993, the member countries completed their move toward a single market and agreed to participate in a larger common market, the European Economic Area, established in 1994.

The EU, headquartered in Brussels, Belgium, reached its current member strength in spurts. In

© BCE ECB EZB EKT EKP 2002

© BCE ECB EZB EKT EKP 2002

© BCE ECB EZB EKT EKP 2002

© BCE ECB EZB EKT EKP 2002

The euro, the EU's currency

1973, Denmark, Ireland, and the United Kingdom joined the six founding members of the EC. They were followed by Greece in 1981, and Portugal and Spain in 1986. The 1990s saw the unification of the two Germanys, and as a result, East Germany entered the EU fold. Austria, Finland, and Sweden joined the EU in 1995, bringing the total number of member states to fifteen. In 2004, the EU nearly doubled its size when ten countries—Cyprus, the Czech Republic, Estonia, Hungary, Latvia, Lithuania, Malta, Poland, Slovakia, and Slovenia—became members.

THE EU FRAMEWORK

The EU's structure has often been compared to a "roof of a temple with three columns." As established by the Maastricht Treaty, this three-pillar framework encompasses all the policy areas—or pillars—of European cooperation. The three pillars of the EU are the European Community, the Common Foreign and Security Policy (CFSP), and Police and Judicial Co-operation in Criminal Matters.

QUICK FACTS: THE EUROPEAN UNION

Number of Member Countries: 25

Official Languages: 20—Czech, Danish, Dutch, English, Estonian, Finnish, French, German, Greek, Hungarian, Italian, Latvian, Lithuanian, Maltese, Polish, Portuguese, Slovak, Slovenian, Spanish, and Swedish; additional language for treaty purposes: Irish Gaelic

Motto: *In Varietate Concordia* (United in Diversity)

European Council's President: Each member state takes a turn to lead the council's activities for 6 months.

European Commission's President: José Manuel Barroso (Portugal)

European Parliament's President: Josep Borrell (Spain)

Total Area: 1,502,966 square miles (3,892,685 sq. km.)

Population: 454,900,000

Population Density: 302.7 people/square mile (116.8 people/sq. km.)

GDP: €9.61.1012

Per Capita GDP: €21,125

Formation:
- Declared: February 7, 1992, with signing of the Maastricht Treaty
- Recognized: November 1, 1993, with the ratification of the Maastricht Treaty

Community Currency: Euro. Currently 12 of the 25 member states have adopted the euro as their currency.

Anthem: "Ode to Joy"

Flag: Blue background with 12 gold stars arranged in a circle

Official Day: Europe Day, May 9

Source: europa.eu.int

PILLAR ONE

The European Community pillar deals with economic, social, and environmental policies. It is a body consisting of the European Parliament, European Commission, European Court of Justice, Council of the European Union, and the European Courts of Auditors.

PILLAR TWO

The idea that the EU should speak with one voice in world affairs is as old as the European integration process itself. Toward this end, the Common Foreign and Security Policy (CFSP) was formed in 1993.

Pillar Three

The cooperation of EU member states in judicial and criminal matters ensures that its citizens enjoy the freedom to travel, work, and live securely and safely anywhere within the EU. The third pillar—Police and Judicial Co-operation in Criminal Matters—helps to protect EU citizens from international crime and to ensure equal access to justice and fundamental rights across the EU.

The flags of the EU's nations:

top row, left to right
Belgium, the Czech Republic, Denmark, Germany, Estonia, Greece

second row, left to right
Spain, France, Ireland, Italy, Cyprus, Latvia

third row, left to right
Lithuania, Luxembourg, Hungary, Malta, the Netherlands, Austria

bottom row, left to right
Poland, Portugal, Slovenia, Slovakia, Finland, Sweden, United Kingdom

Economic Status

As of May 2004, the EU had the largest economy in the world, followed closely by the United States. But even though the EU continues to enjoy a trade surplus, it faces the twin problems of high unemployment rates and **stagnancy**.

The 2004 addition of ten new member states is expected to boost economic growth. EU membership is likely to stimulate the economies of these relatively poor countries. In turn, their prosperity growth will be beneficial to the EU.

The Euro

The EU's official currency is the euro, which came into circulation on January 1, 2002. The shift to the euro has been the largest monetary changeover in the world. Twelve countries—Belgium, Germany, Greece, Spain, France, Ireland, Italy, Luxembourg, the Netherlands, Finland, Portugal, and Austria—have adopted it as their currency.

Single Market

Within the EU, laws of member states are harmonized and domestic policies are coordinated to create a larger, more-efficient single market.

The chief features of the EU's internal policy on the single market are:

- free trade of goods and services

- a common EU competition law that controls anticompetitive activities of companies and member states

- removal of internal border control and harmonization of external controls between member states

- freedom for citizens to live and work anywhere in the EU as long as they are not dependent on the state

- free movement of **capital** between member states

- harmonization of government regulations, corporation law, and trademark registration

- a single currency

- coordination of environmental policy

- a common agricultural policy and a common fisheries policy

- a common system of indirect taxation, the value-added tax (VAT), and common customs duties and **excise**

- funding for research

- funding for aid to disadvantaged regions

The EU's external policy on the single market specifies:

- a common external **tariff** and a common position in international trade negotiations

- funding of programs in other Eastern European countries and developing countries

COOPERATION AREAS

EU member states cooperate in other areas as well. Member states can vote in European Parliament elections. Intelligence sharing and cooperation in criminal matters are carried out through EUROPOL and the Schengen Information System.

The EU is working to develop common foreign and security policies. Many member states are resisting such a move, however, saying these are sensitive areas best left to individual member states. Arguing in favor of a common approach to security and foreign policy are countries like France and Germany, who insist that a safer and more secure Europe can only become a reality under the EU umbrella.

One of the EU's great achievements has been to create a boundary-free area within which people, goods, services, and money can move around freely; this ease of movement is sometimes called "the four freedoms." As the EU grows in size, so do the challenges facing it—and yet its fifty-year history has amply demonstrated the power of cooperation.

Europe is proud of its "bright idea," a union with economic and political power.

The EU believes that it can use its power to act as a "lighthouse" for the rest of the world.

KEY EU INSTITUTIONS

Five key institutions play a specific role in the EU.

THE EUROPEAN PARLIAMENT

The European Parliament (EP) is the democratic voice of the people of Europe. Directly elected every five years, the Members of the European Parliament (MEPs) sit not in national **blocs** but in political groups representing the seven main political parties of the member states. Each group reflects the political ideology of the national parties to which its members belong. Some MEPs are not attached to any political group.

COUNCIL OF THE EUROPEAN UNION

The Council of the European Union (formerly known as the Council of Ministers) is the main leg-

islative and decision-making body in the EU. It brings together the nationally elected representatives of the member-state governments. One minister from each of the EU's member states attends council meetings. It is the forum in which government representatives can assert their interests and reach compromises. Increasingly, the Council of the European Union and the EP are acting together as colegislators in decision-making processes.

EUROPEAN COMMISSION

The European Commission does much of the day-to-day work of the EU. Politically independent, the commission represents the interests of the EU as a whole, rather than those of individual member states. It drafts proposals for new European laws, which it presents to the EP and the Council of the European Union. The European Commission makes sure EU decisions are implemented properly and supervises the way EU funds are spent. It also sees that everyone abides by the European treaties and European law.

The EU member-state governments choose the European Commission president, who is then approved by the EP. Member states, in consultation with the incoming president, nominate the other European Commission members, who must also be approved by the EP. The commission is appointed for a five-year term, but can be dismissed by the EP. Many members of its staff work in Brussels, Belgium.

COURT OF JUSTICE

Headquartered in Luxembourg, the Court of Justice of the European Communities consists of one independent judge from each EU country. This court ensures that the common rules decided in the EU are understood and followed uniformly by all the members. The Court of Justice settles disputes over how EU treaties and legislation are interpreted. If national courts are in doubt about how to apply EU rules, they must ask the Court of Justice. Individuals can also bring proceedings against EU institutions before the court.

COURT OF AUDITORS

EU funds must be used legally, economically, and for their intended purpose. The Court of Auditors, an independent EU institution located in Luxembourg, is responsible for overseeing how EU money is spent. In effect, these auditors help European taxpayers get better value for the money that has been channeled into the EU.

OTHER IMPORTANT BODIES

1. European Economic and Social Committee: expresses the opinions of organized civil society on economic and social issues

2. Committee of the Regions: expresses the opinions of regional and local authorities

3. European Central Bank: responsible for monetary policy and managing the euro

4. European Ombudsman: deals with citizens' complaints about mismanagement by any EU institution or body

5. European Investment Bank: helps achieve EU objectives by financing investment projects

Together with a number of agencies and other bodies completing the system, the EU's institutions have made it the most powerful organization in the world.

EU Member States

In order to become a member of the EU, a country must have a stable democracy that guarantees the rule of law, human rights, and protection of minorities. It must also have a functioning market economy as well as a civil service capable of applying and managing EU laws.

The EU provides substantial financial assistance and advice to help candidate countries prepare themselves for membership. As of October 2004, the EU has twenty-five member states. Bulgaria and Romania are likely to join in 2007, which would bring the EU's total population to nearly 500 million.

In December 2004, the EU decided to open negotiations with Turkey on its proposed membership. Turkey's possible entry into the EU has been fraught with controversy. Much of this controversy has centered on Turkey's human rights record and the divided island of Cyprus. If allowed to join the EU, Turkey would be its most-populous member state.

The 2004 expansion was the EU's most ambitious enlargement to date. Never before has the EU embraced so many new countries, grown so much in terms of area and population, or encompassed so many different histories and cultures. As the EU moves forward into the twenty-first century, it will undoubtedly continue to grow in both political and economic strength.

Xlendi Bay

7 MALTA IN THE EUROPEAN UNION

On May 1, 2004, Malta entered the EU with nine other new member states: the Czech Republic, Estonia, Cyprus, Latvia, Lithuania, Hungary, Poland, Slovenia, and Slovakia. Before gaining membership, each of these countries had to demonstrate a stable democracy, a consideration for human rights, protection of minorities, and a highly functioning *market economy*. Upon its entrance, Malta, with a population of less than 400,000 people, took Luxembourg's previous place as the smallest of the EU's member countries.

Malta originally submitted its membership application to the Council of the European Union in July 1990. The council gave Malta the go-ahead at the Helsinki European Council in December 1999.

On March 8, 2003, a referendum was held in Malta on the question of whether it should become an EU member; 143,094 votes were cast in favor of joining the EU, while 123,628 votes were cast against it. Malta then became a member of the EU on May 1, 2004.

Malta's entrance into the EU was not unexpected, because its membership was a continuation of its involvement in European politics. For example, in 1964, Malta joined the United Nations, and it has since offered such concepts to that body as the Common Heritage of Mankind and the Protection of the Global Climate. Malta also joined the Council of Europe in 1965, and has since added the European Convention of Human Rights to its own laws. Finally, Malta's armed forces have participated in the OSCE since that organization's beginning. Malta's armed forces have served in Bosnia-Herzegovina and Georgia.

Since Malta's acceptance to the EU, efforts have been made by the other member states to raise Malta's economy closer to the level of the rest of the EU nations. Therefore, 38 million euros were allotted to Malta from the EU between

Harvesting salt

Ta Pinu Church

2000 and 2005. This money was used for customs, taxation, education, agriculture, technical assistance, and the environment, to name only a few of its projects.

Malta faced many challenges during its struggle for its EU membership. In 2003, it ranked second in concern of the EU among countries who were preparing to become members. Issues of concern to the EU included animal waste disposal, nature protection, and antidiscrimination laws.

However, Malta has also been envisioned as a new, exciting tourist destination for its other EU member states—"the Mediterranean Switzerland." It is the most racially diverse of all European nations, with historic trading ties to Arab countries and to North African nations. Its many priceless historical artifacts make the entire island an open-air museum of 4,000 years of human history.

In 2008, Malta plans to switch its currency from the lira to the euro to encourage even more investment of world nations in Malta's economy, and also to encourage trade with other nations. To adopt the euro as its currency, Malta has had to keep its own currency stable and level in value with the euro for two years within a designated time-period, a goal that it has already achieved. It will join twelve of the other twenty-five EU countries that have also adopted the euro as their common currency.

Malta has been allotted five votes in the European Union Parliament, out of 230 to 235 total votes of the twenty-five countries combined. The Labor Party, whose candidates have won three of Malta's five seats, worries that Malta's cultural,

Maltese citizen

social, and economic identity might be swallowed up within such a huge community. Some Maltese also fear job losses for the citizens of Malta as the country restructures to meet both EU regulations and a newly competitive business environment.

Malta's citizens are enthusiastic participants in the democratic process. Their almost 85 percent voter turnout in their first EU election was the highest of any of the twenty-five EU countries. While some Labor Party members, most of whom voted against Malta's EU accession, warn that EU policies were never meant for an island country as small as Malta, most citizens of the island see its new EU membership as a challenge that will end with large long-term benefits for its citizens.

A Calendar of Maltese Festivals

Throughout the year: In Guarda reenactments of historical military parades in Fort St. Elmo in the city of Valletta are held. This began during the time of the Knights of St. John, and today includes ninety military officers in costumes enacting real historical events.

February: February is **Carnival** time in Malta, a colorful celebration that occurs five days before the beginning of Lent. It is celebrated with extravagant parades and parties in the large city of Valletta, but it is also present in most small towns, as participants dress in costumes and masks. This celebration began on the islands in 1470.

March: March 9 through 12 is the **Mediterranean Food Festival** in Valletta. This yearly celebration features four days of ethnic music and food presented in the atmosphere of a traditional Maltese village.

April: Holy Week celebrations are held in cities throughout the country. These include **Maundy Thursday** pilgrimages, **Good Friday** pageants, and **Easter Sunday** processions. The Wednesday following Easter is the **Feast of Saint Gregory**, celebrated with a two-mile procession from Tarxien to Zejtun. The celebration originally gave thanks to God for halting the bubonic plague, which killed 11,000 islanders in 1675.

June: June 28 and 29 is the **Feast of Imnaja**, also called the Feast of St. Peter and St. Paul. This event takes place in Burkette Garden, the only wooded area on the islands, and it opens the summer season. Visitors eat traditional dishes of rabbit stew cooked in wine, and listen to traditional folk music.

September: Victory Day is celebrated September 8. This day originally recognized the victory of the Knights of St. John over the Turks in 1675, although it now celebrates many of Malta's military victories throughout history. There is a huge rowing regatta in the Grand Harbor at Valletta.

October: The **Historic Cities Festival** is celebrated October 6 through 16. It focuses on the historic towns and cities of the island. It is especially celebrated in Mdina, Valletta, and Rabat, with music, costumes, concerts, and theatrical performances.

RECIPES

Bigilla
(a traditional dip)

Sold in country villages and by street vendors, bigilla is best eaten with crackers or toast.

Ingredients
1 pounds dried beans
1 chili pepper
1 tablespoon chopped marjoram and mint
crushed garlic to taste
1 tablespoon olive oil
salt and pepper to taste

Directions
Soak dried beans for 12 hours. Add salt and bring to a boil. Simmer until beans are tender. Mash the beans and add the other ingredients.

Kwarezimal
(a traditional sweet to eat during Lent)

Ingredients
14 ounces ground almonds
5 ounces self-raising flour
5 ounces castor sugar*
2 tablespoons of cocoa
rosewater
honey
chopped almonds to decorate

Directions
Mix together the ground almonds, flour, sugar, and cocoa. Add the rose water and enough water to make a soft mixture. Form into a thick patty and flatten until it is about 2 inches thick. Place on a greased baking sheet and bake in a moderate oven at 375° F for 15 minutes.

Remove from the oven and brush with honey. Sprinkle chopped almonds on top and return to the oven for another 10 minutes. Remove from oven, cool, and store in an airtight container.

*If you can't find castor sugar (sometimes spelled caster) in your market, you can substitute superfine sugar. Or, you can make your own. Take regular sugar and grind in a food processor for about 1 minute.

Timpana
(macaroni in a pastry case)

Serves 6

Ingredients
1 pound of flaky pastry
1 pound of macaroni
1 pound of minced meat, a mixture of beef and
    pork
1 large onion
2 tablespoons of tomato paste
4 tablespoons grated Parmesan cheese
1/2 pound ricotta cheese
salt and pepper
1 cup water
1 beef bouillon cube
4 eggs
butter or oil for frying

Directions
The Sauce: Fry the onion until golden in butter
or oil or a mixture of both. Add the minced
meat, salt and pepper. Stir well and cook for 15
minutes. Add the tomato purée and 1 cup of hot
water together with the bouillon cube. Simmer
for at least an hour. Boil the macaroni in plenty
of salted water until barely tender. Pour one cup
of cold water into the pan as soon as the macaroni is done. It is vital that the macaroni remain
pretty stiff so that it will retain its shape. Mix the
meat and tomato mixture into the macaroni, add
the beaten eggs and the cheeses together with
salt and pepper to taste. Stir well. Roll out half
of the pastry to fit the bottom and sides of a

cake tin or oven dish. Put in the macaroni mixture. Finally, cover the top with a pastry lid and
bake in a moderate oven for 1 hour or until the
pastry is browned.
    You will find that this dish slices better if it is
allowed to stand for about half an hour after
being taken out of the oven. The ideal slice has
neat see-through circles of macaroni on both
sides.

Figolla
(Easter Cake)

This cake is flat, very sweet (although this depends on the amount of sugar you use), and is usually cut in forms of hearts.

Ingredients
18 ounces flour
9 ounces butter or margarine
26 ounces castor sugar*
juice and rind (yellow part only) of 1 lemon
vanilla extract
2 eggs, beaten well
evaporated milk

Directions
Pastry:
Rub butter well into flour until mixture looks like fine bread crumbs. In a separate bowl, mix together the eggs, sugar, vanilla extract, and lemon rind. Add gradually to the flour and butter, making sure that they have incorporated well before each addition. Add the lemon juice and gradually add enough water to make a soft dough. On a lightly floured surface, roll the pastry into a ball. Wrap in plastic wrap and refrigerate for at least 2 hours before using.

Filling:
7 ounces ground almonds
7 ounces castor sugar*
2 ounces chopped almonds
1 egg white
water

Directions
Mix together the ground almonds, chopped almonds, and the sugar. In a separate bowl beat the egg white until stiff then add to the almond mixture along with enough water to make a soft paste. Roll out the pastry on a floured surface until about 1/4-inch thick. Using a pastry cutter cut out each heart twice. Place some of the almond mixture onto one of the hearts, leaving a margin of about 3/4 inch all around. Brush this margin with some evaporated milk and sandwich the second heart onto the first, sealing it with your fingers. Brush with milk and place onto a greased baking sheet. Bake in a hot oven at 400°F until browned. When cooled you can decorate with either chocolate or more traditionally with icing.

Pastizzi
(Ricotta cheesecakes)

Ingredients
Pastry:
14 ounces flour
water
pinch of salt
2 ounces soft shortening
2 ounces margarine

Filling:
14 ounces ricotta
4 eggs
pinch of salt
pepper

Directions
Place the flour and a pinch of salt in a mixing bowl. Add a small amount of water. Using an electric mixer on medium speed, combine the flour and enough water to make a stiff dough. Process until smooth. If the dough is sticky, add additional flour, a little at a time.

On a lightly floured surface, roll the pastry out to a 1/8-inch thickness. Use your hands to cover the entire top with the shortening. Roll as for a Swiss roll. Roll out the pastry again. This time spread the top with margarine. Roll as before.

Make the filling. With a fork, mash up the ricotta. Add salt, pepper, and unbeaten eggs. Mash the ricotta with a fork, add the salt and unbeaten eggs.

Roll out the pastry and cut into 3 1/2-inch circles. Place a tablespoon of the filling in the middle of the circle. Top with another circle, and seal the edges. Place on an ungreased cookie sheet. Bake in a 400° degree oven for 20–25 minutes, or until risen and golden brown.

Project and Report Ideas

Map

- Make a map showing the topographical features of the islands that make up Malta.

Reports

- Write an essay comparing and contrasting the workings of the U.S. government with the workings of Malta's government. Within the essay, compare the governments of the two countries with charts and/or diagrams.
- Research and write a brief report on how Malta has changed since becoming a member of the EU.
- Using information found in this book, as well as the library and the Internet, write a story about the life of a young person in Malta.

Projects

- Choose one period of Malta's history that is interesting to you. Research that period on the Internet. Tell about the highlights of your period in a two-page illustrated story.
- Choose four or five of the most important events from Malta's history. Research those events on the Internet or at the library. Make your own illustrated time line of those events.
- On the Internet, look up news articles from the last year and chart Malta's progress as a member of the EU.

Group Activities

- In groups of four students, construct models of the historic cities of Malta, showing four or five examples of the architecture of different historical periods.
- Divide into two groups of three students each, and debate Malta's membership in the EU. One side take the pro-EU membership side and the other the anti-EU membership position.

CHRONOLOGY

5000 BCE	The first human settlers arrive on Malta.
3600–2500 BCE	Megalithic temples are constructed.
800–480 BCE	Phoenicians rule Malta.
480–218 BCE	Carthaginians rule Malta.
218 BCE	Roman rule of Malta begins.
60 CE	St. Paul the Apostle is shipwrecked on Malta.
395–870	Byzantines rule Malta.
454	Vandals occupy the islands.
464	Goths occupy the islands.
870–1090	Arabs rule Malta.
1091–1194	Normans rule Malta.
1194–1266	Swabians rule Malta.
1224	Arabs are expelled from Sicily and Malta.
1282	Malta's residents rise up against French rule; they revolt again in 1798.
1283–1412	The Aragonese rule Malta.
1530	Knights of St. John of Jerusalem take possession of Malta.
1798	Napolean Bonaparte takes over the islands.
1800	British rule of Malta begins.
1914–1918	World War I is fought; Malta becomes known as the "Nurse of the Mediterranean."
1919	Self-government is granted under British rule.
1934	Maltese and English become official languages of the islands.
1939–1945	World War II occurs, and Malta is bombed by Italy and Germany.
1964	Malta becomes an independent, sovereign nation under the British Commonwealth.
1970	Malta enters into an agreement with the European Economic Community.
1974	Malta becomes a republic.
1990	Malta submits application for membership to the European Union.
2002	The European Union formally invites Malta to become a member state.
2003	Maltese voters approve membership in the European Union.
2004	Malta officially joins the European Union.

FURTHER READING/INTERNET RESOURCES

Abela, A. E. *A Nation's Praise: Malta: People, Places and Events: Historical Sketches*. Valletta, Malta: Progress Press, 1994.

Balm, Roger. *Malta [The American Geographical Society—Around the World Program]*. Blacksburg, Va.: McDonald and Woodard Publishing Co., 1996.

Pace, Roderick. *EU's Enlargement Towards the Mediterranean, Cyprus and Malta*. London: Taylor and Francis, 2004.

Friggieri, Oliver. *Koranta and Other Short Stories from Malta*. Rome, Italy: Minerva Publications, 1994.

Goodwin, Stefan. *Malta, Mediterranean Bridge*. Westport, Conn.: Bergin and Garvey, 2002.

Holland, James. *Fortress Malta: An Island Under Siege 1940–43*. New York: Hyperion, 2003.

Sheehan, Sean. *Malta [Cultures of the World Series]*. New York: Benchmark Books, 2001.

Travel Information

www.aboutmalta.com
www.maltaholidayguide.com
www.travel.yahoo.com/p-travelguide-191501774-malta_vacations-i
www.visitmalta.com

History and Geography

www.malta.cc/history.htm
www.malta.com/history.html
www.malta-gozo-info/malta-history.htm
www.nationsonline.org/oneworld/malt.htm
www.searchmalta.com/dir/History

Culture and Festivals

www.aboutmalta.com/ARTS_and_ENTERTAINMENT/MUSIC/FESTIVALS
www.britishcouncil.org/ro/malta-arts-culture.htm
www.discover-malta.com/culture

Economic and Political Information

www.eupoliticstoday.com/malta
www.searchmalta.com/bookstore/trade.shtml
www.uam.es/otroscentros/medina/malta/malpolgen.htm

EU Information

europa.eu.int/

Publisher's note:
The Web sites listed on these pages were active at the time of publication. The publisher is not responsible for Web sites that have changed their addresses or discontinued operation since the date of publication. The publisher will review and update the Web-site list upon each reprint.

FOR MORE INFORMATION

Embassy of Malta
2017 Connecticut Avenue NW
Washington, DC 20008
Tel.: 202-462-3611

Permanent Mission of Malta in New York
249 East 35th Street
New York, NY 10016
Tel.: 212-725-2345

U.S. Department of State
2201 C Street NW
Washington, DC 20520
Tel.: 202-647-4000

U.S. Embassy in Malta
Development House, 3rd Floor
St. Anne Street
Floriana, Malta VLT 01
Tel.: 356-256-4000

GLOSSARY

archipelago: A large group of scattered islands.

autonomous: Able to act independently.

baroque: A style of art or architecture that emphasizes dramatic effects and elaborate ornamentation.

bastions: Large, projecting parts of forts.

blocs: United groups of countries.

capital: Wealth in the form of property or money.

carob trees: Mediterranean evergreen trees in the pea family.

cisterns: Tanks for catching and storing rainwater.

constitution: The written rules and regulations by which a country is governed.

coralline: Relating to or resembling coral.

damask: A richly patterned fabric.

desalination plants: Facilities that remove salts or other chemicals from sea water or soil.

electoral: Relating to elections.

excise: A government-imposed tax on goods used domestically.

executive: The branch of government charged with implementing legislative decisions.

feudal: Relating to the legal and social system of medieval Europe, in which vassals held land from lords in exchange for military service.

frescoes: Paintings on fresh moist plaster, often on a wall, with pigments that have been dissolved in water.

grotto: An artificial structure that has been made to resemble a cave.

judiciary: The branch of government concerned with justice.

lapis lazuli: A deep blue gemstone, often with flecks of pyrite.

legislative: The branch of government responsible for writing and passing laws.

literacy rate: The number of people within a specific place who know how to read and write.

market economy: An economy based on free trade rather than government regulation.

megaliths: Very large stones used in prehistoric architecture.

Neolithic: A period beginning around 10,000 BCE marked by the beginning of agriculture and of using polished stone tools.

parliamentary democracy: A form of government in which people elect representatives to the parliament, the supreme government body.

plague: A disease that spread very rapidly, infecting large numbers of people, killing many.

ratified: Officially approved.

referendum: A decision or measure put to a vote of the entire eligible population.

republic: A form of government in which citizens elect representatives to act on their behalf.

semiconductors: Materials found in most electronic devices that conduct electricity partially but not totally.

Semitic: Relating to the language group that includes Arabic, Hebrew, Amharic, and Aramaic.

solidarity: The act of standing together, presenting a united front.

stagnancy: A period of inactivity.

tariff: A government-imposed tax on imports.

INDEX

PICTURE CREDITS

BIOGRAPHIES

AUTHOR

Having grown up on a farm in southern Virginia, James Stafford now lives on the Southern Tier of New York State with his wife and daughter. He teaches writing and literature at Elmira College.

SERIES CONSULTANTS

Ambassador John Bruton served as Irish Prime Minister from 1994 until 1997. As prime minister, he helped turn Ireland's economy into one of the fastest-growing in the world. He was also involved in the Northern Ireland Peace Process, which led to the 1998 Good Friday Agreement. During his tenure as Ireland's prime minister, he also presided over the European Union presidency in 1996 and helped finalize the Stability and Growth Pact, which governs management of the euro. Before being named the European Commission Head of Delegation in the United States, he was a member of the convention that drafted the European Constitution, signed October 29, 2004.

The European Commission Delegation to the United States represents the interests of the European Union as a whole, much as ambassadors represent their countries' interests to the U.S. government. Matters coming under European Commission authority are negotiated between the commission and the U.S. administration.